KU-251-195

Eggs and Chicks

Fiona Patchett
Designed by Josephine Thompson
and Nicola Butler

Illustrated by Tetsuo Kushii and Zoe Wray
Bird consultant: Dr. S. James Reynolds
Reading consultant: Alison Kelly,
Roehampton University

Contents

Parents and chicks

All birds lay eggs which hatch into chicks.
Most birds take care of their chicks as
they grow.

Penguin chicks stay close together to keep
warm. Their parents stand nearby.

Building a nest

Most birds build nests to keep their eggs safe. They use things they find nearby to build them.

This puffin collects grass to fill its nest.

A bird brings twigs to a tree. It uses its beak to join them together.

It adds moss, roots and grass, and makes them into a cup shape.

The bird presses down to make a hollow in the nest.

Chaffinches can make 1,300 trips a day to collect things for their nests.

Unusual nests

Nests can be many shapes and sizes. Some birds have very clever ways of building nests.

A tailorbird makes a row of holes around a leaf.

It sews the leaf shut with cobwebs, then fills it with feathers.

A hummingbird's nest is tiny. It is made from cobwebs and plants.

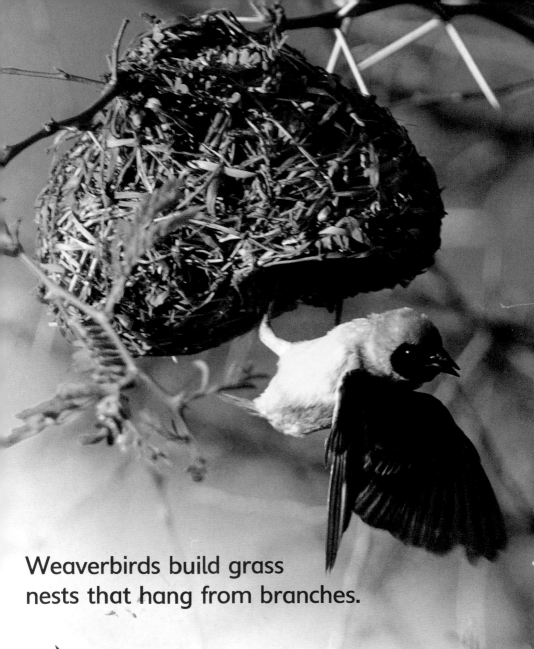

Weaverbirds build grass
nests that hang from branches.

Cave swiftlets make
their nests from spit.

Laying eggs

Some birds don't lay their eggs in a nest. They lay them in different places.

Guillemots lay eggs on cliffs. Their eggs are pointed.

If an egg is pushed, it rolls in a circle. It does not roll off the cliff.

Black skimmers lay their eggs on sandy beaches.

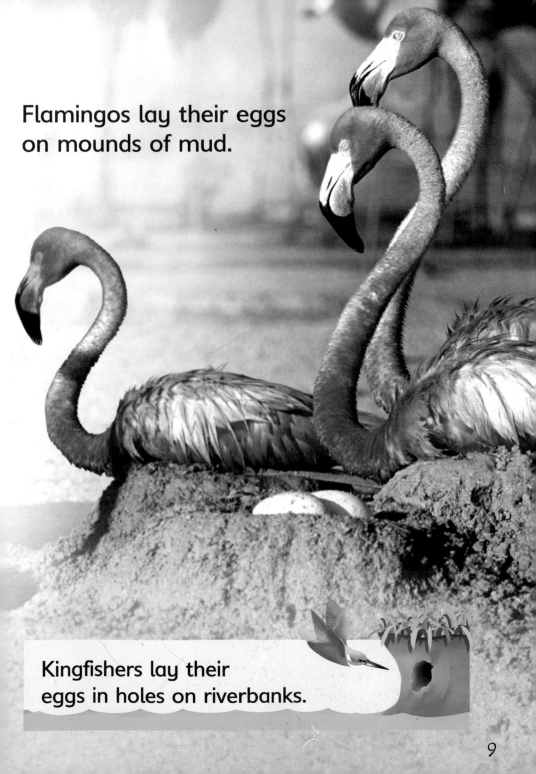

Flamingos lay their eggs
on mounds of mud.

Kingfishers lay their
eggs in holes on riverbanks.

Keeping warm

Birds need to keep their eggs warm so a chick can grow inside.

An emperor penguin balances its egg on its feet. Its body keeps the egg warm.

Penguins balance their egg on their feet for two months.

Mallee fowls bury their eggs under soil and leaves. The leaves rot and give out heat, which keeps the eggs warm.

A bird may lose feathers on its chest.

The bare area helps keep its eggs warm.

Inside an egg

When an egg is laid, a chick starts to grow inside.

The red spot on the yolk starts to grow into a chick.

Yolk

The yolk contains food which helps the chick to grow.

Chick

The chick grows bigger. The white protects the chick.

White

8

Chicks take from 10 days to 75 days to grow inside an egg.

The chick grows to look like a tiny bird with a beak, eyes and feet.

A chick cheeps inside its egg. Its parents can hear its call.

Hatching

When a chick is strong enough, it hatches from its egg.

Egg tooth

1. A chick has a lump on its beak called an egg tooth.

2. It uses its egg tooth to make holes around the shell.

3. The chick pushes the top off the egg, then rests for a while.

4. The chick struggles out of the shell. Its feathers are damp.

The chick's feathers dry
and become fluffy.

The chick doesn't need its
egg tooth. Soon it drops off.

In the nest

Chicks born in nests have thin feathers. They stay in the nest until more feathers grow.

1. Chicks are born with closed eyes.

2. Feathers start to grow on their bodies.

3. After a few days, their eyes open.

4. Soon the chicks don't fit in the nest.

These egret chicks have to grow stronger feathers before they can leave the nest.

Cuckoo chicks

Some cuckoos don't build nests. They lay their eggs in the nests of other birds.

A cuckoo lays its egg in another bird's nest and flies away.

The bird sits on the nest and keeps all the eggs warm.

When the cuckoo hatches, it pushes out the other eggs.

Cuckoo chicks call again and again so adult birds will bring them more food.

A cuckoo chick is often bigger than the adult bird which feeds it.

Dinnertime

Chicks need lots of food to help them grow.
They eat things like insects, seeds or fish.

Fairy terns feed their chicks with fish.
The chick swallows the fish whole.

Some chicks try to push
other chicks away to get
the most food.

A mother arrives with a worm. Her chicks open their mouths.

She pushes the worm into a chick's mouth and flies off for more.

A chick's mouth is very bright inside. This shows its parents where to put food.

First flight

Chicks know how to fly when they hatch, but they need to be strong before they leave the nest.

Chicks try flapping their wings a lot.

When their wings are strong, they jump from the nest.

They stretch their wings and glide to the ground.

Some birds ignore their chicks
so they have to leave their nest
to look for food.

This baby fairy tern
is flapping its wings,
but it can't fly until its
feathers have grown.

Good parents

Birds take care of their chicks until they are big enough to take care of themselves.

Swans carry their chicks on their backs. Baby swans are called cygnets.

Male swans scare animals away from their cygnets by puffing up their feathers.

Some chicks hide
in their mother's
feathers to keep safe.

In hot places, birds have to
keep their chicks cool.

An emu uses its
body to protect its
chicks from the sun.

A shoebill showers
its chick with water
to keep it cool.

Growing up

Baby birds learn how to take care of themselves by watching their parents.

These houbara bustard chicks are learning how to hunt for food by watching their mother.

Chicks copy the songs their parents sing.

Chicks follow the first thing they see. It is usually their mother.

If they see another animal, they think that animal is their mother.

Ducklings know how to swim as soon as they hatch. They don't need to learn.

Different eggs

Some eggs are plain and some are speckled.
There are lots of shapes and sizes of eggs.

Plovers lay their
eggs among stones
on beaches.

The eggs are speckled.
They are hard to spot
among the stones.

When the chicks
hatch, they are hard
to spot too.

Arctic
tern egg

Kestrel
egg

Blue-winged
pitta egg

American
robin egg

All these eggs are their actual
size. This ostrich egg is the
biggest kind of egg.

Hummingbird
eggs are the
smallest.

American golden
plover egg

Glossary of bird words

Here are some of the words in this book you might not know. This page tells you what they mean.

 nest - a place that birds build to keep their eggs and chicks safe.

 yolk - the yellow part in the middle of an egg. It helps the chick to grow.

 hatch - when a chick breaks out of its egg through the shell.

 egg tooth - the part of a chick's beak which it uses to break the egg shell.

 cygnet - a baby swan.

 duckling - a baby duck.

 speckled - covered with little dots that make a pattern.

Websites to visit

You can visit exciting websites to find out more about eggs and chicks.

To visit these websites, go to the Usborne Quicklinks Website at **www.usborne-quicklinks.com** Read the internet safety guidelines, and then type the keywords **"beginners eggs and chicks"**.

The websites are regularly reviewed and the links in Usborne Quicklinks are updated. However, Usborne Publishing is not responsible, and does not accept liability, for the content or availability of any website other than its own. We recommend that children are supervised while on the internet.

Index

Acknowledgements

Managing editor: Fiona Watt, Managing designer: Mary Cartwright

Photo credits

The publishers are grateful to the following for permission to reproduce material.
Cover GettyImages/Tim Flach and Andy Sacks **p1** GettyImages/Laurie Campbell. **p2-3** Windrush Photos/David Tipling. **p4** Kevin Shafer/CORBIS. **p6** Michael and Patricia Fogden/CORBIS. **p7** Warren Photographic/Kim Taylor. **p8** Dan Guravich/CORBIS. **p9** Nature Stock Shots/Mary Helsaple. **p10** Robert Schoen/Still Pictures. **p11** Bruce Coleman/John Canalosi. **p13** (top) Robert Pickett/CORBIS, (bottom) Julie Habel/CORBIS. **p15** Stockbyte. **p17** GettyImages/JH Pete Carmichael. **p19** Martin B. Withers/CORBIS. **p20** © Malie Rich-Griffith/infocusphotos.com. **p21** Christian Decout/Still Pictures. **p23** Roland Seitre/Still Pictures. **p24** Philip Perry/CORBIS. **p25** Bruno Pambour/Still Pictures. **p26** Xavier Eichaker/Still Pictures. **p27** FLPA - Images of Nature © Minden Pictures. **p29** © Natural History Museum, London. **p31** Stockbyte.

Sun, moon and stars

 Farm animals

 Elizabeth I

 Rubbish and Recycling

 Dogs

 Horses and ponies

 Spiders

 Planes

 Cats

 Ancient Greeks

 Volcanoes

 Dinosaurs

 Your Body

 Armour

 Sharks

 Celts

 Vikings

 Castles

 How flowers grow

 Digging up the past

 Living in space

 Caterpillars and Butterflies

 Ballet

 Pirates

 Egyptians